Time Pieces

for
Viola

Music through the Ages in Two Volumes

Volume 1

Philip Bass and Paul Harris

The Associated Board of
the Royal Schools of Music

CONTENTS

Time Pieces for Viola

Volume 1

c.1360 Personent hodie

Anon. (German)

AB 2816

1551 Basse danse bergeret

from *Musyck Boexken*

Tylman Susato
(*c.*1510–*c.*1570)

1582 Divinum mysterium

from *Piae cantiones*

Anon.

1612   The Earl of Salisbury's Pavan

William Byrd
(c.1540–1623)

1686 The Twenty-Ninth of May

from *The Dancing Master*

John Playford
(1623–1686/7)

1687 **Siciliana**
from Sonata No. 6 in A minor

Gottfried Finger
(*c*.1660–1730)

1689 Riggadoon

from *The Second Part of Musick's Hand-maid*

Henry Purcell
(1659–1695)

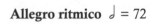

*c.*1700 Noël nouvelet

Trad. (French)

1725 Alle Menschen müssen sterben

BWV 262

Johann Sebastian Bach
(1685–1750)

The title of this chorale can be translated as 'All men are but mortal'.

AB 2816

1728 If the heart of a man is depressed with cares

John Gay*
(c.1685–1732)

from *The Beggar's Opera*

Fine

D.C. al Fine

*Although commonly attributed to John Gay, the music to *The Beggar's Opera* may have been composed (at least in part) or arranged by Johann Christoph Pepusch (1667–1752), the conductor of the first performance. As is typical for a 'ballad opera', many of the work's songs or 'airs' use popular tunes of the day.

1740 Under the Greenwood Tree

Thomas Arne
(1710–1778)

from *As You Like It*

1778 Theme from Andante grazioso

from Piano Sonata in A, K. 331

Wolfgang
Amadeus Mozart
(1756–1791)

c.1810 Ecossaise

WoO 23

Ludwig van Beethoven
(1770–1827)

AB 2816

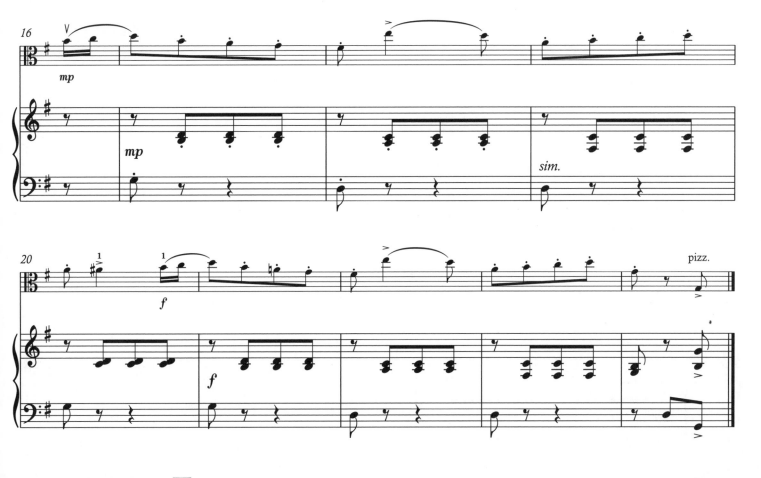

1823 Entracte

from *Rosamunde, Fürstin von Zypern*

Franz Schubert
(1797–1828)

1867 Arietta

from *Lyric Pieces*, Op. 12

Edvard Grieg
(1843–1907)

1878 Mélodie antique française

from *Album pour enfants*, Op. 39

Pyotr Tchaikovsky
(1840–1893)

AB 2816

1893 Larghetto

from Sonatina in G, Op. 100

Antonín Dvořák
(1841–1904)

1908/9 Jeering Song

from *For Children*, Vol. 1

Béla Bartók
(1881–1945)

* In the original piece for piano the metronome mark is ♩ = 160.

AB 2816

1914 Theme from 'Jupiter'
from *The Planets*

Gustav Holst
(1874–1934)

1917 Menuet

Maurice Ravel
(1875–1937)

from *Le tombeau de Couperin*

Allegro moderato ♩ = 92

sourdine [una corda]

3 cordes [tre corde]

1963 Charade

Henry Mancini
(1924–1994)

2000   Viola Joke!

Paul Harris

Printed in England by Caligraving Ltd, Thetford, Norfolk

Music origination by
Barnes Music Engraving Ltd, East Sussex